Text by Christina Goodings
Illustrations copyright © 2013 Amanda Gulliver
This edition copyright © 2013 Lion Hudson

Published by Lion Children's Books
an imprint of
Lion Hudson plc
Wilkinson House, Jordan Hill Road,
Oxford OX2 8DR, England
www.lionhudson.com/lionchildrens

ISBN 978 0 7459 6366 2

First edition 2013

A catalogue record for this book is available
from the British Library

Printed and bound in China, November 2012, LH17

My Own Little
Easter Story

Christina Goodings

Illustrated by Amanda Gulliver

LION
CHILDREN'S

The children waved palm branches.

"Hooray," they cried. "Here comes Jesus, riding to Jerusalem!"

"Hooray for God's chosen king."

8

Jesus went to the Temple. It was festival time. People had set up a market.

Jesus tipped the market stalls over.

"Get out of here," he told the stallholders. "This place is for prayer, not for making money."

Another day, Jesus watched wealthy people bringing gifts of money to the Temple.

A poor woman gave two tiny coins.

"The priests have it all wrong!" Jesus told his friends. "They say long prayers, but they don't care about what God wants.

"They told that woman to give money, even though it was all she had."

The priests were angry about Jesus.

"But people love the things he says and does," they agreed. "How can we catch him?"

Then Judas Iscariot arrived. Jesus had chosen him as one of his twelve friends, but Judas had a wicked plan.

"If you pay me, I'll tell you where to catch Jesus alone," he told the priests.

The time came for the festival meal. Jesus shared a meal with his twelve chosen friends.
He passed them the cup of wine.
He broke the bread.

"When I am gone, share a meal like this,
and remember me," he said.
"And love one another."
Judas simply slipped
away.

After the meal, Jesus and the others went to
the olive grove where they planned to sleep.
As Jesus was praying, Judas came back.

Armed men grabbed Jesus.

"The priests have questions," they told
him.

The priests asked their questions. It was clear Jesus hadn't done anything wrong. But the priests had already made up their minds.

In the morning they took Jesus to the Roman governor, Pontius Pilate.

"This man is a troublemaker," they said. "You must punish him."

Pilate gave in to what they wanted. He ordered his soldiers to crucify Jesus.

From the cross, Jesus said a prayer to God: "Father, forgive them."

Jesus' friends stood a little way off, weeping.

As evening came, friends came and took
Jesus' body. They laid it in a tomb. They
rolled the heavy stone door shut.

Then they went away. It was time for the
weekly day of rest.

Early on the Sunday, some women returned to the tomb. They wanted to say a proper goodbye.

To their amazement, the door was open. The tomb was empty.

Two angels appeared. "Jesus is not here," they said. "He is alive again."

But was he really? No one had seen him.
One of the women, Mary Magdalene,
stood by the tomb weeping.
"Why are you crying?" asked a voice.

Mary turned. "You must be the gardener,"
she said. "Have you seen Jesus?"
The man said her name: "Mary."
Then she knew. It was Jesus!

After that, Jesus appeared to the good
friends who still believed in him.

"Soon I will go to heaven," he told them.
"I want you to go on doing the work
that I began:

"Tell people about God's love. Show them how to live as God's friends."
And the message of God's love is the message of Easter.